Wix

Professional Websites Created in Minutes

(A Comprehensive Guide to Building Your First Website With Wix)

Ronald Higgs

Published By **Jordan Levy**

Ronald Higgs

Wix: Professional Websites Created in Minutes (A Comprehensive Guide to Building Your First Website With Wix)

ISBN 978-0-9958936-3-4

No part of this guidebook shall be reproduced in any form without permission in writing from the publisher except in the case of brief quotations embodied in critical articles or reviews.

Legal & Disclaimer

Table Of Contents

Chapter 1: Website Development

Web design is the art of creating a website. Coding, designing, writing and designing may all be part of this. In order to create a site web designer can cooperate with others within the field, such as web developers.

Developers can create Windows Installer, Microsoft's installation engine for installers, using their WiX toolset. It's accessible to anyone, and is open source and backed through the.NET Foundation. WiX is a set of software that can be used to create Windows Installer packages, such as .exe configuration bundles,.msi installations packages,.msm combine modules, and. MSP patches employ similar build concepts like the rest of your application. Automated build systems can employ the WiX command-line tools for building. Additionally, in addition to accessing them through the command line Visual Studio and Team Build are compatible with MSBuild. WiX includes a variety of add-ons to enhance the functionality of the program to extend beyond Windows Installers. As an example, WiX can install Internet Information Services (IIS) websites as well as develop SQL Server databases, and include firewall-related exceptions to Windows.

It is the WiX Bootstrapper Burn can be used to make setup bundles which include your software and all needed dependencies like the.NET Framework, and various runtimes. Through Burn you can combine multiple downloaded programs into one executable file. Furthermore, the writing of codes that are compatible using Windows Installer, such as customized actions written that are written in C# and C++ is made easy by using the WiX SDK's native and managed libraries.

It is common to start building a website according to a certain need or need. One example is that a person might need to share the latest information, market wares or offer services. The process of designing a website can begin once they've determined the purpose of their site. It is important to determine what data will be displayed on the website and how it will be displayed. It is also important to consider what elements that the site will need and the way users interact in interaction. Web designers can create the design of an online site after the initial design has been established. The colors, fonts and images must be considered. It is also important to think about the overall design of the website and the way each page is connected to each other.

When the graphic layout is complete, construction can begin. For websites, developers use markup languages such as HTML, CSS, and JavaScript to bring their concepts into reality. Though it isn't easy there are a variety of tools available to help make the process feasible. The site is up for testing and observing what it does in real life will be the next thing to do after the programming is done. With time, and as technology advances along with when emerging user needs are uncovered Web designers might need modify and update to their websites.

Overview of Wix

An effective online presence is vital to running an effective business regardless of the industry. It helps in promoting brand awareness in business development, mobilization of employees, and global expansion. Limiting your business to some geographical limits means you're prepared to lose thousands of potential clients as well as endless opportunities to grow. For a strong online presence, you'll require an individual website that can be expensive based on features, the number of websites, and price of the designer. When I first started my site I was worried about the cost of the custom-designed website as well as how the web designer could provide me with the features I wanted. There is a lot of time and effort is involved in creating a website which is why I was eager to have a successful outcome. I was not aware that about the Wix site that lets you create your own website completely absolutely nothing. Although it might seem odd, but it's exact.

Wix is the one-stop solution to create your own custom site without having to hire a web designer. It's a breeze to use and once you've created your site, you're ready to launch it instantly. Additionally, it's SEO-friendly, which means you won't need worry regarding your website's ranking in search outcomes.

The process of building a website can be difficult and lengthy in case you've not used this method previously. It can take a long time for the site to load that can be frustrating when you have to get something accomplished quickly, however your system is slow. Try to develop some patience in the meantime. For you to start making your own website, initially sign up for and then create an account. It is then possible to download, alter and then distribute your stored documents. So, you are able to begin the same place you left off when developing your site at any point and not have to begin with a new site. Along with handling payment and invoices, it also shows latest bundles, coupons, as well as the domain's control panel.

Wix offers mobile-friendly website templates. Sites that function properly on mobile devices can be designed. In fact, that's an advantage. It's a feature that you will appreciate. This allows more flexible communication between your organization's various places. When you launch a site the first step is to choose one of the templates, choose the title of your site, and alter the individual pages. It's that simple. If you're seeking to create an online presence without having to hire an expert designer, Wix is a solid alternative to take into consideration. It may take time to master how to utilize these tools effectively, once you've mastered it the basics, it's easier to put into place the ideas you have for your website.

The use of Wix templates

Wix it was first introduced in 2006, has revolutionized the world of web-based development. Wix came up with a strong and user-friendly platform that allows people to be creative and to have fun, without having to master the intricacies computing. Wix is a simple web editor that is loaded with options and tools to make the process of launching and running a successful online enterprise.

Digital hubs can be customized and equipped with links to quick information, fast-loading data guidance, etc.

An Editor was designed to aid you in creating a visually unique and feature-rich website that will appeal to your visitors. It's simple and fast and allows you to present your message with the most engaging and captivating way possible. It's our goal to offer you an interface that's simple enough to not need "a getting used to" to be able to utilize it efficiently. Additionally, the editor allows the direct personalization of your site to match the preferences of your users. In this instance, neither programming skills nor artistic limits are needed.

Your site can be assured that your site will be safe when hosted by Wix. Applying powerful online Apps and Services will help your business and its website grow. The design of your website is flawless on any screen size. Mobile site conversion with one click Available today. The personalization of your domain can be a great option to wow your site's users. The creation of a stunning and efficient web page for your organization is easier than it has ever been with the aid of a simple one-page design. The latest features, applications as well as design templates will be added frequently. If you're a photographer music lover, owner of a business or entrepreneur, Wix offers everything you require to build a stunning web page.

Help Center which can answer your queries

In the case of online sales, a sleek professional website is crucial. If your site (and consequently your business) isn't trustworthy nobody will purchase from you via the web. Therefore, make sure your site is updated and highlights your best work. Your website will be found by customers when they can locate your site using search engines such as Google. The process of optimizing search engines (SEO) is dedicated to improving the visibility of a site's website on result pages of search engines. While it might seem daunting at first, it is possible to take several steps that will give your website the greatest possibility of making it up the ranks of the search results on Google. Find out more information about the importance of search engines optimization (SEO) for your online store by studying Wix's Blog. Wix Blog.

The information on how you can promote the products we offer can be located at Wix's Blog. Wix Blog. It is important to treat your product as an actual service must be taken into consideration. Review reviews of actual customers concentrate on the benefits as well as drawbacks to using the product. They are a reflection of the value they've received from your product, as well as their levels of satisfaction. When you take note of their comments it will build a stronger relationship to them above the level of transaction. You develop into a sympathetic helper. Advertising that is effective considers a quality of the product and its significance to its intended audience. Take a look at the wonderful experiences that your customers will experience with your product and make use of those experiences as a source of inspiration for your advertisements.

It is essential to have an instruction manual that guides you through all aspects of marketing before you start your own firm. You can also sign up to an established website that frequently publishes in-depth tutorials and tips on marketing for smaller firms. The Wix Blog is a must to subscribe. Wix Blog first and foremost however, you must be sure to keep. Discover more about your area of expertise through reading blogs as well as other online resources pertaining to your needs.

A website is the start of a successful presence on the internet. It's about keeping things up and running, finding new clients, as well as marketing the ones you already have. The majority of potential customers to make a judgment about your business after having seen just your site. The visual appeal of a website goes beyond mere pixels. Wix has made it easy to arrange your contact details within the My Account part of the website and allows you to quickly connect with your clients. The Wix ShoutOut app lets you deliver relevant content, promotional offers and coupons to the people who are most interested in your brand. Wix allows you to create and share coupons vouchers, discounts or other promotional offers to your clients using ShoutOut, email, as well as social media.

The Wix platform lets you quickly establish a set of automated emails that will be delivered to anyone who makes an initial purchase through your store. Because Google has begun penalizing sites that don't have a mobile-friendly design use, Wix Mobile editor Wix Mobile editor is a excellent way to please both the customers and Google.

Want more people to discover your fantastic site?

The increase in your website's SEO is the only method that is effective to increase visitors to your site. Do you even know? It appears that the Wix team has taken this into consideration also. In order to make sure that all your website's SEO requirements are in place Try using an SEO Wizard. Its SEO Wizard will crawl the site and present a detailed easy-to-read report to improve the search engine ranking of your website.

The appeal of web design lies in its variety and there's no single way to create a distinctive web page. In the case of designing a website possibilities of making an amazing thing are nearly limitless, because of the many devices available. Beautiful images accompany written content that is well-written. If you're willing to play around with your Wix editor you also, are able to achieve this look with a range of boxes, pictures, and colors. Checking that everything appears on the page exactly precisely where it is supposed to be can be a straightforward way to enhance the aesthetics and performance. Affixing your web pages' elements is an excellent method for achieving this objective. Wix allows you to arrange elements on your site. The Wix Editor allows you to align elements on your website. an already-designed grid is accessible for you to use.

The primary aspect to operating a website is the management of the SEO.

Promoting your website online is something you could accomplish. If done properly, SEO can catapult your business onto the first page of Google and attract clients in a flurry. It is possible to improve your website's SEO by giving each page a with a concise, simple and clear title.

Logos are a great method to provide your company with an appearance that is professional as well as improve the settings for search engine optimization. In this instance, the site's title in Google search results can be referred to as the Google title, or Meta Title in search engine optimization. Secured password protected pages as well as other methods that make certain sections on your site not accessible by search engines (also called "non-indexed" in search engine optimization) are excellent methods to safeguard sensitive information. Additionally, because Google is blind to images by nature, providing a descriptive alt-text description for every image enhances the ability of Google to crawl the contents of your website, and thus improves its SEO.

As customers search the internet to find companies similar to yours, crawlers search the internet to find terms that relate to the services you offer. Each of your site's pages have a reason for being there. Be sure to highlight specific words in the name and contents of your internet pages in order to emphasize the purposes. Wix is friendly to users, but most businesses do not have the funds to differentiate their sites. By obtaining this accreditation Web administrators who are Wix experts can apply their knowledge effectively and may also reward them financially.

Wix offers cheap hosting services for its entire websites Customers can also benefit from them by choosing the right one. Additionally, web designers who collaborate with Wix.com as well as similar platforms can expect to provide cheaper prices than those who have custom-coded sites. In addition, clients can easily understand how to manage their website with Wix because it's simple to use. It is possible to make changes without the need to pay an expert programmer to do everything. Customers with a smaller budget that want to have a professional site could get the benefit of having Wix. Wix designer.

What makes it better-known than other products similar to it?

Wix is the largest and most well-known web builder as it allows you to create professional static sites and takes control of your extravagant Flash web design ideas. While Wix is able to transform any boring website into a stunning static work of art it is more popular for people to go to a vibrant and striking Flash design website. This means that artists and photographers will finally be able to showcase their work using the way they want to. Furthermore flash is a great tool for portfolios. Flash style gives any portfolio style your best.

Chapter 2: Simplicity of Operation

Wix is a web-based website building tool which requires none technical skills for the user. One of the major reasons Wix is so popular is due to its easy drag-and drop interface. Furthermore, Wix makes it easy to design static websites, and lets you incorporate Flash as the main feature. Through the combination of Flash and Wix developers can create beautiful, professional-looking sites quickly. A lot of people, specifically those looking to show the world their artwork and photography use Flash due to its numerous advantages. The flexibility of Flash's design and appearance is a major feature that makes the platform a popular choice. Numerous business owners have opted to Wix for revamping their websites to boost traffic and increase sales.

Cost Effectiveness

Wix is a simple to use site builder tool that won't cost you a fortune. It lets you upload your existing site that many web designers have to implement. Furthermore, Wix is quite reasonably priced due to the many plans offered. The prices for these plans are around $20 per month. eCommerce can be relatively inexpensive and easy to set up. But, the advantages may differ based on the goals you have for your website. The website's success is enhanced by the low cost and short education curve. Also there is a coupon included in order to help in reducing the price.

Numerous Samples Available

One of the major issues faced by earlier website builders is the demand for better quality templates that they can work with. The wide range of Wix's readily available templates is among its major advantages. If you're starting a business or simply creating a personal web site it is possible to select among hundreds of templates available. If you're trying to figure out how to build a site and are interested in learning more how to do it, this is a great opportunity to take a break. People can take their time perusing the templates available to find ideal one for the requirements of their site. Additionally, there are no hidden costs or costs are associated with making use of the templates provided.

Wix has proved extremely useful to those who require more technical knowledge who wish to build websites or enhance existing ones by incorporating Flash elements. But, some users were unhappy that they couldn't get access to all the options if they bought an upgrade. The ability to access these slots does come at an cost but is worthwhile over the long term. This being the sole negative aspect, it's difficult to think of anything more to critique.

Features

Wix offers a wide array of additional tools and features to help you build your site. The web editor of Wix sets it ahead of the pack because it grants you greater control over the design and experience of your website than other web builders. Additionally, Wix boasts the largest range of Flash styles among all website builders, whereas many of its competitors are stuck within the realm of static sites.

Wix lets you add various types of content on your website. This includes PayPal, Google Maps, clip art, media players as well as videos from websites such as YouTube. One could argue that it would be difficult to create your perfect site with everything you have available. However, you'd be mistaken. Drag-and-drop editors ensure that you'll be able to finish your item within a matter of minutes. The well-organized user interface of Wix allows users to easily access all the editing tools available. Change the images that are left on the screen and the layouts to the right side, after that, review and save your work in the upper right-hand corner of the display. The process of creating a website hasn't been simpler.

Pricing

Amazing as it sounds as it may sound, you do not need to cover any of these mentioned before! You pay nothing for hosting and you can utilize all of the templates you wish, and use Google Analytics and use 500 megabytes of storage space and bandwidth. You also have four additional options, which range in cost starting at $4.95/month with My Domain to $24.90/month for the My Domain plan to $24.90/month for the more expensive eCommerce plan. These funds are used to pay for bandwidth, storage as well as the shopping cart. Additionally, Wix provides professional customer support even for users who are not paying as well as the site has been designed to work with the search engines such as Google.

Making choices about the templates

After you've selected the type of template that you want to be in, the website offers you access to a multitude of template designs that you can alter to meet your specific needs. After you've chosen the appropriate template, you can easily to modify the background image and color to meet the needs of your.

What's the point of WiX?

The .wxs extension for files is utilized to store WiX source code. WiX source code which can be written using XML. WiX instruments use a traditional link and compile method for converting sources into executable codes. These WiX Source files will be compared against the standard WiX schema during the build phase and then an editor, preprocessor and linker run them through. In the end, various types of output can be produced using the diverse WiX tools.

Specifications for technical specifications of WiX

WiX operates with.NET 3.5 in addition to versions 4.0 or higher. MSBuild, the software used in WiX, requires.NET 3.5, which isn't available within Windows 8 or later versions of Windows Server. The development with.NET 3.5 won't be supported once WiX v3.11 comes out; consequently, a change to.NET 4.0 is crucial.

Wix is a web-based platform that has many advantages.

Wix is a free website creator that's been making headlines among potential business owners as it makes establishing websites for promotion simpler. There are over 200 themes that you can choose from accessible, and users with an artistic inclined can start from beginning with a blank slate and come up with something original. The themes are varied and can be classified into a number of categories including: Business eCommerce, Real Estate music, personal, and real estate. The loading time for the first page is less than a minute, and websites can be built in just a few only a couple of minutes. In this post We'll go over Wix's numerous advantages and explain how it might be suitable for your needs. The numerous benefits of the tool include:

Reasonable Prices

The free version comes with a few limitations, however it lets users to test whether Wix will work to your business prior to committing to pay for the service. The most basic annual plan will cost you around $4 a month. The monthly plan is available at around $5 monthly. Attaining the top monthly goal cost just $20 a month and offers unlimited storage traffic, storage space, and the ability to access technical assistance prioritised.

Simplicity of Operation

It was previously mentioned that it is possible to select from more than 200 pre-designed designs in order to help you get an idea of the overall appearance and experience of your site. we've found that this may help to eliminate any confusion that you might have. In addition, Wix's easy interface and the absence of the need for any technical expertise makes editing your website a breeze.

Integration is Easy With Wix the ability to connect numerous apps, like Google Analytics, without sacrificing its ease of use.

Efficient Use of Keywords

In the absence of proper SEO Search engines and users are likely to overlook the best constructed web page. It is possible to make your Wix website more easily accessible to crawlers of search engines with the help of keywords or other data. Be sure, however, that you use the efforts put into the creation of your website carefully.

Levels of Challenge

Wix is able to make use of its features by establishing a difficulty level for each design that it provides. Therefore, those who are new are advised to stick with the basic templates. Those that have more experience can look at more advanced or intermediate choices. Due to this, people of any experience are able to feel secure making use of Wix.

Updates

The process of editing and updating content can be an overwhelming task However, Wix takes away the burden through making it easy. Its user interface is straightforward and allows you to alter your website as you need to without any exertion.

Exemples that are formalized

Wix is an excellent option if you don't have the creative talent but wish to come up with stunning design ideas for your site. There are more than 500 amazing professional, contemporary, and well made templates are provided. They are easy to edit You just need to change the data in the templates with the images, text and various other elements. Most of them use HTML as their base. Therefore, they're optimised to be viewed by the search engines. This means that getting ranking on the web for your site is quite simple. Additionally, you can choose from numerous attractive layouts that are flash-based available for you.

Chapter 3: An abundance of apps available

Nearly every app related to websites that you can think of is offered within Wix. Nearly every website-related app you could want is available in Wix App Store. All the apps you can think of to include Google maps, surveys and even a shopping cart can be found there. Shop around and choose the item you're most interested in. You can get certain features for no cost, while other options require the price of. Make use of paid upgrades when you're able to pay for them, however stay with the core functionality in case you're strapped for cash.

It's very simple to operate

Like we said previously that the interface of Wix is as easy as drag-and-drop. Pick the material you want (be it an image or a textual content, or even a slideshow) and drag it wherever you'd like. A slideshow will show the latest layout of the site before your eye. This is a time and labor-saving.

Support

There are many things that could go wrong anytime within the internet world, which is why it's crucial to have a security net that is in the right place. Wix is a great tool for security. Wix team has been accessible all hours of the day and night this is a great benefit for users. Additionally, you can get assistance from their agents by calling them directly. It is a unique option to set the time for a callback session with an Wix professional to your own convenience. Reach out to Wix's experts if you encounter issues on the site or have a question. If they are unable to assist them directly, they'll guide you to the correct direction. There are numerous resources that can assist you in your learning.

Version for free

People often want to test things before buying it. Wix provides a no-cost version which includes the entire set of tools needed for creating a website that has a the professional look.

The creation of websites is made using the Wix editor

In the case of creating websites, Wix is an excellent alternative since it does not require any programming knowledge to be learned on your own. There are many pre-designed templates and designs to select from, or make your own completely entirely from the ground up. Wix can also allow you to incorporate websites as well as contact forms on your site. An extensive discussion of the subject matter is available in the chapter on contact forms.

The Art of Website Development

Wix is a site builder that provides its users with many customization and customizing options. With Wix it is possible to start by scratch or make use of the many of their pre-designed themes. When you're in need of a web site, Wix makes it simple to build one that's attractive and performs efficiently. Don't simply start writing something new, you need to pick a good template before you start. Wix offers users numerous high-quality templates that you can choose. Once you have selected a template you are able to modify it satisfy your requirements. In particular, you can change the colors, fonts, and layout so that it reflects the style of your business.

Additionally, the site created using Wix could be enhanced using numerous useful tools. You need an online shop today! That's fine, it's not an problem. Wix simplifies the process to start a shop on the internet. In addition, they have strong capabilities to handle SEO creating and disseminating forms and many other things. Wix is able to assist however you think suitable for your site.

Developing a Reliable Website for Your Business

An attractive website can fulfill multiple purposes, such as advertising, selling items or services, showing off skills as well as connecting with people and increasing brand recognition. It's as if you have a launchpad to take your business to space and take over the globe. In this post we will go over the steps involved in creating your site from beginning through. Also, I'll pay careful focus on branding and marketing basics to make sure your website is both functional and attractive.

How do you build a trustworthy web site:

Design your brand's strategy

Make sure you have a clear and consistent plan for branding that is applicable to every aspect of your site starting from your primary goal to the fundamental principles that govern style and tone. If you follow the steps below, all of them should become evident:

Find out who you want to reach:

They, who?

What ethnic and racial groups do they represent?

What is it that they enjoy doing? How do they perceive themselves

What effect will your website or brand will have on people's lives?

Find out about the firms within your field.

Find out about the market through research of rivals to find out their tactics, weaknesses as well as opportunities.

Branding involves the process of articulating distinctive characteristics

If you could summarize your company in a few phrases What are they? What's the primary reason that drives your brand in the first place? Then, consider your brand's personality and pinpoint its distinct characteristics, like its color scheme, lexicon and its aesthetic.

Content that is consistent with the brand

This is the perfect right time to start getting down to work and begin creating the material that will appear on your website as well as in other brand assets. The first step is to create your brand's identity. This includes an image, logo video, slogans, and other written content. All of these elements should match the brand's image and add to the overall strategy for branding.

Get in Touch With the Design

A professional website design includes a lot of elements to consider, from choosing the perfect color palette, to creating the ideal layout. It's true that creating your own website with an empty template is feasible with a little experience and knowledge in web development. However, if you're worried over the amount of time required to create a site and you'd rather save a bit hours you can use Wix to create a stunning web page in three simple steps:

Select an existing model, or make use of ADI to serve as a starting place.

What You See Is What You get (WYSIWYG) Website builder software like Wix removes the requirement to memorize and learn codes to create websites. Wix provides its users with an established base in the creation of websites, using customizable templates for websites. There are a variety of professionally-designed websites themes, styles and styles. Choose the one most suitable to your idea regardless of whether it's the site for personal use as well as an online store or a different site. It is ideal that the template you pick is already designed in a manner that meets your requirements and helps you achieve your goals. It is also possible to have Wix's ADI build your website and then make changes afterward.

It's worthwhile to modify the template in order to match the other elements of your website. Wix suggests using JPEG, PNG, and GIF images to ensure they appear at great on your website So, make sure to include those files initially. Use the editor's theme and site style to refine the design and ensure it is consistent to your branding. It can be as straightforward or as complex as you like. Check out the following three examples of stunningly constructed websites created with Wix templates. Be aware of the various ways the basic templates have been modified to make unique web pages!

Customize the template for your website.

Change the design Make sure you use the best designs, colors, and images are only the beginning of designing your website. There are a number of media elements in order to enhance your site's overall design. You can, for example, think about adding background animation or videos on your site. Add depth to your website by adding motion or parallax scrolling.

Prioritize usability

Anyone who is interested in your site must be attracted to your site but they need to be kept exploring it is also necessary provide an enjoyable customer experience. Your website will not be successful if it is beautiful websites that are non-functional. Be attentive to these crucial aspects while creating an effective web site:

Coordinated Navigation Flow

Sites that are simple to navigate include ones with layouts as simple and as simple as is possible. Additionally, the website's menus and internal linking structures must make it easier to allow visitors to switch between various sections on the website.

The sequence of content

Seven of the main guidelines of design is the hierarchy. It is therefore essential to make the entire attention to. If people come to your website it is important that they be guided by a way that meets the needs of your business. Thus, you must ensure that the top features of your site are in the front in the center when designing your layout. In addition, you can make use of color, size, and placement in order to highlight important details within your layout, in line with this set of guidelines. If, for instance, you would like people to sign up to your product, make sure you highlight the button for subscription. Effective usage of the content hierarchy can be evident on this landing page that outlines the process to start a blog with large headings as well as prominently positioned buttons.

Calls-to-action

A call-to-action (CTA) refers to a concise message that encourages site users to complete a certain action. Utilize phrases such as "Register Free," "Get Your Toda," and "Subscribe" to entice site customers to do something. They will make clear to your visitors the things you would like they to complete and create confidence about what happens once they hit an action.

Readability

The ability to read text in a typeface is a fundamental notion. Make sure you use legible fonts in size that is readable, and font colors that pop against backgrounds and allow your text plenty of room to breathe by incorporating appropriate quantities of white space.

Footer

The footer of your website refers to the part of your website which is located at the lower part of the page (the top of the page is known as heading). The users may not pay any at all to the footer however, it has many functions to improve your site's user-friendliness. Consider, for instance, adding a footer that includes your contact details and a social media buttons. As well as a short overview of who you are as well as what the site's content is including a site disclaimer and a simple website map that includes links to all your webpages, you can make the following changes.

Get yourself ready for a search engine.

One of the most efficient ways to improve traffic is to increase your website's ranking in search results. That's why SEO or search engine optimization (SEO) must be an absolute priority right at the beginning in the development process for your company's website. The search engines optimization (SEO) is becoming an vital aspect of a the digital marketing plan. The key elements comprise:

Keeping track of trends for keywords

Consider things from the viewpoint as a potential client or a site-visitor. What could be some possible Google questions that may be bringing them to your site? Search engine optimization efforts must be guided by search terms that people type into their searches. Utilizing tools for keyword research can help you determine the keywords you should be targeting.

Text

It is recommended that you took into account SEO or search engine optimization (SEO) when writing web-based content including the menu, the FAQ page as well as the blog, footer or bio sections. There are numerous ways to boost your site's SEO. But, among the most essential actions you can take is to find natural and tasteful ways to integrate your keywords in the content. Google's algorithm is very sophisticated, and it could punish your website if it seems as if it's an advertisement.

Metadata

Google and the other search engines scrutinize your information. Therefore, you must control the information they show on your site's results. In the end, spending the time to optimize your website as well as helping search engines with getting to know your website is worth it.

Alt Text

Images are vital for your SEO effort also. This is why you must include alt text on every image you upload on your website (short to indicate alternative texts). To websites that use search engine, the alt text can be short sentences that describe the photo. It allows users to locate your photos within search results. That is the reason the inclusion of SEO-friendly alt texts for each image is vital.

Link to the creation

If different websites link to your website, your ranking on the search results will likely increase. Start by adding your site to directories, making sure that your social media profiles are linked to your site and encourage users of your website to share information.

Remember that SEO is an ongoing process that never ends once your site is live. For long-lasting results You must continue to improve your SEO over time.

Create a Site that looks more Professional

Take a look at how your website could contribute to your personal development, besides the primary goal in presenting your company's image or product on the internet. A variety of factors can help enhance the appeal of your website for your intended audience dependent on the nature of your business or area of expertise:

Chapter 4: Calendaring programs

It's a fantastic choice to manage appointments online since it simplifies billing, booking and promoting the services you offer.

Thanks to eCommerce platforms such as Shopify, Bigcommerce, and others, creating a online shop and running it is never easier. But, it is possible to start by starting with nothing but a blank page or select one of our templates to set up your shop online.

A fitness-related community online

It's not enough to just put together a fitness business and expect to have a full solution that incorporates the gym management software, internet payment and booking, as well as flexibility in staffing and scheduling.

The Music Portal

Wix lets you sell your songs online, and keep all proceeds. In the end, you are able to connect with more potential customers without losing control of your music.

Critical software

A variety of useful tools to enhance the capabilities of your website can be located in Wix App Market. Wix App Market. It is possible to, for example utilize a tool that helps track your site's stats, countdown timers for boosting sales, or an attractive text animation that will impress the visitors to your website.

Make adjustments for mobile devices

It is crucial that your website works efficiently on desktop and mobile devices. Research shows that nearly 50% of website visits are from smartphones. Furthermore, as Google has rolled out its adoption of mobile-first indexing sites optimized for mobile get more prominence when it comes to ranking in search engines. It is the reason why you must focus on creating a website that is accessible to smartphones.

With Wix's mobile editor, you can instantly convert your desktop layout mobile-friendly layouts using Wix to create an excellent website. Design and style can be changed to increase accessibility for mobile devices in terms of font size, readability, and navigation. Furthermore, those using mobile devices can access your website by using an app that you design. Wix EditorX is an effective tool for creativity specially designed to cater to agencies and designers, providing users full control over breaks. The tool uses a brand new flexible canvas that permits users to drag and drop easily with a state-of-the-art responsive design. Additionally, it offers the complete freedom to design your website for any screen dimension.

Create interesting content

The most difficult part of operating the best website isn't making the site, it's getting visitors and keeping them. The development of trust and loyalty for your brand through content creation, publication and distribution is the foundation of any effective strategy for marketing through content, and will lay the foundation to create your own content marketing plan. The first step to start your content marketing strategy is by using one of the following options:

Publishing Newsletters

Marketing campaigns via email, similar to newsletters, could increase the number of website visits if they contain pertinent and interesting content that entices the user to take a look. Wix offers everything you require to make a great mail marketing strategy, such as templates that you can modify to suit your needs and marketing automation tools transparent metrics, and many other.

Create a blog right away.

It is beneficial to blog for many motives. You can also attempt to earn money from your blog as it can improve the traffic to your website. A greater number of customers and readers are likely to be drawn to the product or service you offer by writing across a wide range of topics. A blog can allow you to show your level of expertise in your field and also allow you to communicate your ideas and thoughts in a way that is more relatable to the audience.

Be on the lookout for new sites

If you'd like your business's website to be able to handle the increased amount of traffic it'll see, it has to work without issue. Maintenance of your website can be a daunting task and time-consuming, but it doesn't need to be. If you wish to prevent this from happening then you can take some small, easy steps. Such changes could be noticed on the contact page and the replies to customers' feedback, your web-based stock and links as well as the privacy policy. It is crucial to maintain the attention of your customers and keeping the credibility of your website.

Considerations to make when creating a site

Your website's appearance and feels in general is comprised of the layout, colors and fonts.

The type of information you wish to display on your site. It can include images, text, video and more.

What is your site it's for. Are you looking to sell products or services to be sold?

Explain the circumstances. Are you able to generate leads?

Who are you trying to connect with? Who do you think your site is intended to reach?

SEO is also known as Search engine Marketing (SEO). This will ensure that your site appears in search results whenever people search for what you offer.

Your financial plan. What was the amount you spent for the design of your website and its debut?

Great ways of creating an online site on Wix.com

Making an account on Wix. Wix account

Let's get started and find out the answer together. If you visit the website and click on the link to sign up for an account, you'll be presented with the following webpage (or the one that is very similar to it as the designs are always changing):

If you're ready to start, simply select the Start Here button. Next, you must create an account if it's not previously. Please fill out the form using your email address, as well as your password (or you can use the existing Facebook account or Google account, if you wish to). It is possible to sign up with your account's email address and password, or by using the account you have on Facebook account or Google account. The following page will require you to pick one that matches the site you wish to develop.

Deciding on a Template

The website offers a selection of templates editable that you can alter to fit your needs after selecting the category you prefer. You can, for instance, easily alter the background image as well as the color after selecting your style. In addition, adding and deletion of pages is easy. Be aware that you are unable to modify the template after you have finished So, make sure you select the template carefully.

Prior to deciding on a template

When you are choosing a design it is essential to know what you're looking for on the site. In order to move ahead without retracing your steps you should ask yourself some basic concerns.

What's the goal of your website?

Ask yourself what you would like to gain from this website. Perhaps, for instance, do you would like to begin your own blog, sell products or showcase your online CV? Understanding the purpose of your site can assist you to select a style which best represents your idea or business approach.

What kind of site do you want to find?

Although some sites are created to look professional, some are designed to make your experience more entertaining. Thus, it is important to be the first to decide on which message you intend to send. It will be easier by using a professionally developed template. However, remember that you need to consider altering the design of your website so that you are able to differentiate.

Do you have a particular goal that you are aiming regarding your product?

It's important to be clear of the brand you want to build and your goals for getting the best value of Wix. If you do not want to start, you can begin with a small amount and then expand. If you would like your clients to be impressed of your company, selecting the right template to match the aesthetic of your brand is important.

Take a look at the competing Wix websites while building the site you want to build. This way you will be able to discover the strengths and weak points of various internet resources. When you're ready to build your website You can take lessons from the most effective parts and incorporate these into your website to ensure maximal effectiveness. Time

Also, consider what time frame you'll have to create a website. There is a possibility of spending tens or hours constructing your Wix website, for example when you've got lots of time but aren't planning to launch your business or product in the near future. Selecting a template that has the features and look that you'd like to have on your website will help you save time when you have to create an entirely new website within minutes or even days.

If you've got an concept of what you would like your site to achieve then you are able to begin looking through the Wix library of templates for pre-made websites. Explore the collection of images to get more suggestions. With the wide selection available at Wix.com it is possible to find everything you need. Use the search feature (located in the upper left on the template page) to narrow down the perfect match to the needs you have, or are able to browse the results. By clicking the "new" button on the sidebar takes you to the latest template collection. You can also select to link the Most Popular Templates to link under the New Templates option. In the end, if you'd like to build a website by scratch, choose to select the Blank Templates option. If you're still unable to find something that you like then you can narrow the search down by selecting the appropriate category. To see the way that the layout will look when you use a smartphone click on the "Mobile View" icon in the left-hand corner of the screen.

By going through each of the pages, it can provide you with a more clear image of the way that the website could look in normal situations as well as help you comprehend how the templates flow. It is always possible to refer back to the lessons on editing when you're stuck. Be sure to review your browser's settings as particular pop-up add-ons or filters like AdBlock and AdBlock can block your browser from opening the template to edit. When you've settled on the layout and you've selected it, you'll receive an all-screen preview. Click Edit This Website if you believe that this could be a great basis for your web site.

If you notice boxes appear in the templates, then you'll know you're in editing mode. The equipment you'll need to begin making adjustments in the window. The design of your website's background could be changed after you've selected the template. Remember the main point you'd like to repeat over.

The Background

Background can be modified by clicking the icon that is located on the left on the interface of editor. After that, you can click the Image button to upload a background image. Then, you can select a gallery of photos already available or upload your own. It is possible to do this for each page of your website individually and you could apply the same theme for all of your websites in a single click choosing Apply to Other Pages. By selecting "Color" will result in an all-black display. When you add video, you can make use of animated sequences or videos to create the stage. Take care not to make it difficult to focus attention on anything on the webpage particularly the words that are printed immediately on top of a video. When you've uploaded an image to be the backdrop, there are several display options to choose from. Choose the Page background pane's "cogwheel' settings icon to access the controls.

The background image will be scaled to cover all of the display.

You can use this feature to make sure that height and width remain equal to one another.

The background image will be laid out on the display as explained in the name.

"Tile Vertically": This option divides your site's information into tiles that are arranged vertically.

Like the vertical tile layout, however using the image as a horizontal design.

Selecting this option can cause the background image to maintain its original size.

If you want to use the scroll background select the checkbox that will appear right next to the background. Then, you'll be able to give a colour to the area on which your image doesn't operate on based on the display option that you pick (for instance, "original size"). Then, press to click the Change Color button to bring you to the Color Selector.

Do I have the ability to utilize exactly the same Wix background for multiple web pages?

Just two clicks can duplicate your background onto any other website that you enjoy. For the background to be used on multiple pages, simply select the background in the Page Background menu and click apply to other pages button.

Clicking on the button beside All Pages from the Apply to Other Pages menu applies the background change to all pages. This will allow you to improve the performance of your website in general by providing visitors with an enjoyable and engaging experience. Alternately, you can select specific pages on your list by selecting the checkbox beside them. Make sure to click OK before confirming the selection, or choose specific pages or pages that share the same topic.

Controlling Pages

In order to apply your background on other webpages requires two easy steps. If you want to apply the backdrop on other pages, select Apply to Other Pages in the Page Background menu. Then, choose the checkbox beside All Pages in the apply to other Pages. This can be used for adding knowledge to every webpage on your site. You can also select the checkbox on each page of the list of pages. Click"OK" to confirm your choice. Alternately, you can select an individual site for example, those that feature a similar topic. Wix permits you to create the number of pre-designed or empty pages.

Furthermore, you can add, edit from, or change the order of the page listing. Furthermore, Wix allows you to create subpages which will be displayed within your drop-down menus in a snap. The first step is to click Pages: Home drop-down menu to the left side of the editor. Select the + Add Pages option to create more pages. After that, you can click to add in the lower left corner. Following that, select Page and select the layout for your new page by selecting the Page Layouts menu located on the left on the right.

After that, enter a title for the page in Name Your Page. If you select the Add as subpage box, you'll be able to create your page to a subpage. When you're done, hit on OK to close.

In the image to the left side, the terms "Home," "Nature," "Architecture," and "About" refer to preexisting websites which were created after an appropriate category was picked. The style of characters can change based on the font you select. The template can be used page with no modifications, but you can change its name or even delete it, if you prefer. If you select the round icon beside the page's title and you'll be shown the menu below, where you can decide to change the name or remove the page.

Adding Text

Certain websites cannot work without texts. You should provide a summary of who you're and what you're doing in business, and ask users to connect with you should they have queries or suggestions. Keep in mind that text is most appreciated by the search engines, before you start with your content plan. If the content you create is high-quality and is original, it could get higher rankings on the search engine results. To improve editing, spelling checking grammar and more importantly, if create a significant amount of content, and auto-saving when there is an interruption in connection, a lot of users choose to write their content using a separate file like Microsoft Word. Text copied from Microsoft Word can be transferred to Wix.

Hit on the "+ Add" button located on the left of the screen. This will get you going.

A text box is sure to show up since it is the primary feature to include. The menu offers a variety of choices for the size of text and font. If you are already familiar with the particulars of the forms you'll need to create, you are able to alter the settings of the template through editing the properties of the text box. Options for formatting"Site Title" text field "Site Title" text field are listed below. They comprise font size, background color, color and the basic formatting of text. For editing the text within the text box, click twice on the box. Then, should you wish to eliminate the box's text, simply select the box and then press the delete button. If you're planning to delete the item and move your attention to a different part of the page, simply click anyplace outside of the box. Seventy-five thousand character characters (including spaces) is the maximum for one text box.

Adding Images

Your website's images are the ones that will draw interest. So it is essential to handle it correctly. Wix makes it easier to process including, changing the arrangement, or removal of images.

Furthermore, Wix provides access to millions of free editable photos. You can also upload a new image should you wish.

Use the Add button on the left of the editor to add an image. Then, snap a picture using"Shutter. Then, you can choose the image to upload, an image that is a stock photo from any of the available images, or an existing social media account that you can share the photo to (e.g. or a post posted on your Facebook page). When you go to the Add Images page, you could choose a single image or a number of images.

Use the Upload Image button to upload a photo from your personal computer. You'll then have access to your saved images through the open button. In the final step, pick your images in the Add Images menu, and click Add. Once you have uploaded a picture the image will be stored on your account. It will be you can access it through the My Photo Uploads section.

It is possible to select various photos by pressing the CTRL key and clicking on every one. Be aware you are able to increase the size of your photo in.gif ,.png, or.jpg format.

If you want to dispose of a photograph then you can select it by left clicking and press the Delete button on your keyboard. Or, you may right-click to select to delete in the contextual menu that opens.

Gallery Wix

The presence of gorgeous galleries on your site will help get noticed quickly. You can change your gallery at any time you want but you must test different options until you discover the best mix. To start Add the cursor towards the left of the editor. Then, hit the + sign. Once you have done that you will be able to access you will be able to access the Gallery tab can be opened. Be aware it is possible to access Wix App Market Wix App Market also has additional Gallery options that are available on Wix. Take a look at their Change Gallery Type option if you're looking to play around with the design of the website or experiment with various designs. There is no need to download all of the images in your gallery because they'll all be automatically transferred.

Choose a gallery that allows you to switch gallery kinds, then select the drop-down menu to customize the style you prefer. When you've completed it, you'll be able pick the other gallery layout to suit your preferences. Don't worry. The process of removing and adding galleries to the gallery can be done with ease. It is possible to experiment with a variety of designs until you find your preferred style that works most. Be sure to review your site using Preview mode to check what it appears like to your visitors.

Chapter 5: Including a Photo in Your Wix Gallery

Select the gallery you'd like to put the photo, after that, select Change Images from the gallery's context menu. Select Add Images after organizing your gallery's photos. Choose one or more images from the window, then click the add button. If you wish to add more than one image choose the photos that you would like to use. If you are presented with the choice to sort Your Gallery Pics then click the button to complete. There's no limit to the amount of images you are able to upload into the Wix gallery. However, be aware that uploading photos could make your website slower.

Pick the gallery you would like to include your image in then right-click on it and select Settings from the menu which appears. For adding images into your gallery, go into Gallery Settings, then select Organize Images. Choose the Upload Images option once you are there. After that, open your file browser on your PC to upload images, find the picture(s) you want to upload, then open the file. It is possible to arrange your photos within the gallery by simply moving them and dropping them in the preferred position.

It is possible to delete the image from your gallery at one point. The first step is to select the image that you would like to get rid of. Then, click the garbage bin symbol in the Organize Your Gallery Images section. Then, you'll be able to effortlessly make use of Wix.com to control the photos as well as links in case you want to upload any photos in your gallery. Additionally, you have the option of choosing the images you want to display or conceal and also give each a brief description.

Support for embedding external images

Select a photo for connection using the gallery button after which you can select Change Images from the option which appears. Information and links can be added to the pop-up menu. If you'd like to alter your gallery, just go ahead by clicking on the gallery once more, and select the style you want to use.

Wix Strips

Strips can help you split your website into horizontal sections to improve its organizational structure and overall design. By incorporating Strips, you can customize the appearance and add into your site. Choose Strips in the Add menu to the left side of the editor. In the menu you can select a strip, after that, select Settings to modify the background image. After that, pick a picture when you click Add Image, and then Change Images. There are three options to choose from: Actual Size and Fit and Crop options are utilized within the Image Scaling section, much similar to the galleries we discussed earlier. Strips for pre-designed web pages usually come in templates.

Customize

For a change in how your strip appears, go to the strip, and then select Options from the menu. It allows for features like changing between photos as well as titling and explaining each photo in the strip, as well as the effects of transition between images as well as text. It's quite similar to gallery's features. You can also change the appearance of the strip at any point simply by selecting its style within the menu which appears to you. You can play around with the numerous choices to discover the one that is compatible with the overall design and layout.

Wix Boxes

The site's layout can be modified. layout, and split it into various parts with boxes. Design, aesthetics as well as the user experience on your website will gain from this. For a start with the box, visit this section of Add similar to the as you did for the strip. To do this, go to the left-hand side of your editor and click the Add button. It is possible to access the box by clicking the Add button. The package can be noticed by adding media including text, images galleries, films, and more. The contents of your package is affected by the move. Furthermore, Wix helps you to do this to move and drop your items in the boxes. After that, place the item inside the box. With containers, you can mark text, and then separate parts of the background.

Customizing

If you want to alter the appearance of your box Click the box until you pick it up, and then select Change Design from the menu which pops up. Select a style from the drop-down menu that pops up and select OK to save your modifications. If you want to create a brand new class, or to make modifications to an existing class then select Customize Design. There, you can change the existing template and save it to be saved for future uses. Shadows, colors, corners as well as borders could be altered in this section. After you've finished making any adjustments, select OK.

Shapes and lines

The addition of any one of the readily available shapes for your website is easy and easy. Use the + sign on the editor's left side to add an item. Select the desired shape or line by clicking Add and then the concave shape. Lines that are added to the website's design help distinguish parts and enhance the readability of the website.

For repositioning a shape, or cable, simply drag it into a new position after which you click on its paintbrush icon. This will open the Customize Design menu, where you can alter the parameters such as the width of the line and its colour. Check the box beside Maintain Aspect Ratio has been checked in order for the size and width of the design to remain in proportion.

The fill color as well as the border color can be chosen through the respective buttons. In the end, you can modify the border's width by moving the bar of scrolling called Stroke Width. If you want to further alter your design simply click it, select the three diamond shapes adjacent to the Design brush symbol. This will bring to the menu Add Animation.

Wix.com lets you set an online file-sharing service for your site's users easy.

Select the Add button located in the left-hand side of the editor for uploading a image. The appropriate Document Buttons by clicking More. If you select an Add Documents option to select the documents you want to upload by simply dragging them out of a folder to the box. Follow the instructions. Then, you'll be able to Choose Document in the event that you already have the files within your media management. After you've uploaded them the files can be transferred the files to the designated section of your site. Once that is done, guests could. Multiple file formats are available with documents maximum 15MB are able to be transferred.

Videos

Wix.com's editor for websites supports the videos hosted on Vimeo and the video sharing site YouTube. If you embed a video on YouTube it is important to ensure that

that it's available to all users. On the YouTube's Advanced Settings, ensure the Allow Embedding box is selected. Also that the full-screen links isn't working within Wix. Wix player, so not use the feature. The videos HTML codes to insert it, if you're not using one of these applications. Player HD and TubePress are only two of many amazing video programs available through the Wix App Market (see the links below this page).

In order to insert any new content into Editor, select the plus symbol. Then, select the Media menu and select video. In order to embed a video, type in your URL for the video's URL on YouTube as well as Vimeo. Additionally, you can make use of YouTube's Search Videos option to look for videos on YouTube to integrate into your website. Search Videos is where you need to type your search query and click the search button. Select Add after you've found the video you would like to see.

It is important to be distinct to stand out in the sea of video clips on YouTube. The first step is to select the video you want to play. It is possible to alter the URL and hide the controls of the player as well as enable additional features such as autoplay and title bar display and brightness in the Video Settings panel. Furthermore the video's appearance can be altered using Modify Visuals. Once you have adjusted your video, simply click in the box that isn't visible to leave the video Settings window. As with the rest of Wix.com this Video Settings panel gives you ample room for playing in terms of aesthetics. We'll need the URL to the video.

The URL of the video that you typed in when uploading.

Instant playback on page loading: To play automatically on user's entry on the page.

Turning in circles Choose this option if you wish your video to be played continuously. What conditions trigger the flashing of controls? Take away or show the video player's control buttons.

Audio

Choose Add from the left-hand side of the editor's interface. Choose music and explore the available alternative options. Wix Music lets you post your music and embed the player wherever you want on your website; SoundCloud Audio enables you to stream any music you've saved on their site; and Spotify If you've got an account, allows you to stream music from your PC or smartphone.

Navigate to the Share menu on the bottom of the player or song after you have logged in to your SoundCloud account. You will receive an embed code. For further action, open Wix's audio editor and sign in to SoundCloud. Input the code in Embed Code, then click Update, then quit SoundCloud for saving your changes.

Customizing your audio

To alter the settings for the music player you can adjust the settings for the player by clicking on the gear icon then choose the settings you want to use (such as Show image or autoplay) in the menu dropdown. Once you've made the adjustments, simply click beyond the player screen to close the dialog box. Then, double-click on the player. Then, select the Show on every page checkbox if wish to have the song loop continuously throughout your website. Be aware that playing the music isn't quite identical to looping it.

The auto-play feature and the audio button

As an alternative to a fully-fledged musician, wix.com allows you to share music by clicking the "Audio Play" button. It is possible to style it however you'd like. The first step is to go towards the left of the editor, and then click the icon Add. This is where you'll see"Music". Click on it to reveal the "Music" button. Choose between Mini Players as well as the Themed Players (the second that will show a specific type of design for your site) then modify the track using the usual methods that are available on the player's pop-up menu. When you are presented with a pop-up menu select Settings to modify the song.

The user can alter your Auto Play Button by clicking it, then selecting the option in the menu that pops up. Then, press"Autoplay" or click the "Autoplay" or

"Loop" button to turn on the function. It is recommended to adjust the volume at a level that is comfortable. For adjusting the volume, locate the slider under the button. Move the slider left or left or.

Using Buttons

Add buttons to your site, and they will connect to different pages such as documents, email addresses as anchors, documents, or different websites. If you would like to increase the number of people to access your website and visit your site, ensure that they are able to access the information they require. You can select an option for layout is available through the Add. Similar to Media Player, Themed Buttons are shown first and contain suggested actions based on the theme for your site that you select. Naturally, every button could be altered once it has been set in the normal method. These options will be displayed after you click them in the pop-up menu. You can then click the controls that correspond to them and access the controls.

Text Modification: Edit the text displayed when you click the button. The controller may be linked to an external or internal web page, an email address, or even a document. It can set the text's left right, or central alignement in the layout currently being used.

Change the appearance and pick a fresh design.

Make the button move immediately after the web page starts loading with animation. The majority of the time, dials and buttons do not have an actual action.

Chapter 6: Links to web sites documents, emails, or websites

Click the button and from the drop-down menu which appears, select the link which will take you to an external URL. In order to enter the external URL choose Web Address after that. Then, you'll be presented with an option to have the webpage start in a new tab or to keep it open inside the one you're currently in. When you've chosen your option then confirm by choosing Yes. Connecting another one of your pages will work the same way Choose Page, and choose the webpage you want to link to. The word "anchor" is shorthand for how the user's experience should begin when they visit a webpage. Links can be, for example, point an individual to a page's halfway point in order to draw attention to an element of information.

Select "Insert an email address" and then enter the address that you wish to send. The next screen will appear Click Insert, choose the topic and then select the appropriate subject line. In the final step, select"OK. Choose your option, and select a hyperlink from the drop-down list that displays. Then, select the Document option beneath Link To Document. After that, begin a fresh upload, or select the file you already have on your personal computer.

Navigation

The menu for page navigation in the editor can be found when you want to quickly switch between pages. The first step is to click on the Pages icon located in the lower left-hand corner of the editor. You can then choose the drop-down menu you see after you click on the circle just to the right of the name of the page to navigate between your pages.

Rearranging the Text

It can be easily relocated to the desired position from the drop-down menu by simply dragging it off the drop-down menu, and dropping it where you want.

Subpages

The page can be moved to the right by using the drop-down menu. This will make the page part of the page's parent.

Page duplication

Wix.com's page duplicate feature is an efficient time-saving tool that should be employed throughout the process of construction. The following steps should follow when you quote pages. First, select the page you want to quote in the drop-down menu and click duplicate. Then, on the screen you see, type the title of the page before hitting OK.

Page deletion

Furthermore, the option of erase the current page can be found there. If you've made an error on your website and would like to begin again it is possible to remove the page, and restart everything with this feature. Then, you'll be asked "Are you sure you want to delete?" with a pop-up message. The option to delete it is available at any time if you'd like to. In this case it is recommended to use the left "Cancel" button. Make sure to remember that the deletion process is irrevocable!

Page Naming, URL, and Settings

By clicking the Settings link opens the option to configure more options. Every one of your site's configuration choices are listed on this page. There is the option of performing various operations for pages, such as changing the name, hiding or making your home page more appealing, changing keywords, or even changing the page's title (how it appears on the listing of pages) as well as the URL (Remember that when changing the URL, you should make sure that the new address is short and pertinent). Additionally, changing settings on Pages is as easy as switching to a new page.

Selecting a website

Your Wix.com site's homepage should look attractive and appealing. Your website's homepage would be its most visited webpage in a perfect world. It should encourage users to visit the content. When you've settled on the subject you'd like to include as your home page, select it using the Settings drop-down menu at the at the top. After that, you must check the box marked Use this site for my homepage. If you're happy, click the Done button. On Pages, a home icon will be displayed beside the URL of the new homepage in order to show that it's the main homepage.

You may want to protect your site's pages when you're working on the site. But, in the event that you're planning making major modifications to your website the information you have is important at the start. Choose Hide the page on the menu that contains you can see the circle on the menu Pages to ensure that your pages are private.

Change of Page

It is possible that you want to change the transition animations for the pages of your Wix website. It's fairly simple to do. Select the Pages tab located on the left of the editor and make your transitions between pages. After that, choose the proper change within the Page's Page Transitions menu.

If you select None then the pages will alter without animation or any other effect. Pages can be moved horizontally by using

Swipe Horizontal Pages. Its Swipe Vertical Pages feature allows users to switch between pages simply by sliding across in the vertical direction. If you select Cross Fade, the pages slowly change into view. When you choose Out-in, the currently displayed page will go away and then be replaced with the next one.

Landing Pages

If a website is to be productive, it must have users as well as the job of a landing pages is to entice those visitors to complete the action they want by providing contact information or exploring the website further. A landing page that is unique can entice visitors to continue looking around your website. When creating a landing pages pick a layout that is tailored to your requirements. Once you've created your landing page you'll be able to change the design as you'd like.

Incorporating a Landing Page

If a website is to be effective, it requires people to visit it to visit it, and a landing pages' purpose is to get users to take the action they desire which could be giving contact details or digging deeper into the site. Furthermore that having a distinctive page that is a landing point will encourage people to continue exploring the remainder pages on your website. The landing page could collect potential leads, as an example you could have the due Soon or under Construction page.

In order to create a landing pages Choose a layout that you like. Once you've completed that, you'll be able to change the layout as you like. The process of creating a landing page is the same as creating any other type of page. It's also a bit more context for those who want to learn more about this.

Here are the steps to create an effective landing page.

Make a brand new page

Choose the right page.

Select the Show More button.

Select Settings.

Select Layouts.

Choose No Header & Footer.

Select on the Done button.

There won't be any alternatives for navigation on the home page. However, if you have an option that directs visitors to your homepage you can let them explore other pages on your website. For simplicity change the design of your landing page can be accomplished in the same way like editing other pages.

Visibility

There are two methods for users to get to the landing page, if you don't wish to have it appear on your list of navigation options:

This page will be your homepage for your website. Unless you provide a different URL, the entire site's visitors will go to this page.

You can also copy the URL of your page and distribute it with the members of your audience privately via social media channels or ShoutOut. This implies that users go to your site upon clicking on the link instead then being automatically directed to your site.

It is possible to make the website's new landing page as your default homepage by choosing it under your Settings menu. You must first select the checkbox that says Use this site as my primary homepage. If you're pleased, hit the"Done" button. You will see a icon for the house in the Pages section of the brand new website. The same way you will be able to see the URL of the page from the Settings menu. You are able to copy and paste the URL in other areas.

Incorporating a Home Page Hyperlink

It's helpful to have be aware that the landing page you are on does not have the header and footer. In addition, that's the reason why there's no menu option. So, it is recommended to add the button on your site's home page if you wish visitors to be able to navigate different pages swiftly. The good news is that landing pages can be linked directly to your primary site (if you decide to create separate landing pages, naturally).

For the first step, select the option you prefer on the main page. After that, choose link To within the new page that appears. Once the page is displayed following the click then select Page. Next, choose your home page in the Link to Page drop-down box (it will have the navigation bar so that users are able to access all other pages) Click"OK" to finish the process.

It is easy to include a menu on your landing page by choosing Add in the familiar menu bar and then choosing the menu that you wish to include. The title of each accessible pages on your website will be displayed on the menu which you will shift to wherever you like. Selecting it, and selecting Settings can allow personalization.

Password Security

It is possible to protect your password on particular websites. Use this only on the places you'd like to secure, because it restricts access to all users. The protection of your site's passwords is a thing we suggest. It's good news that Wix has the capacity to accomplish this. Visit Page Settings to quickly password-protect some websites.

To password-protect a page:

Choose the Pages tab from the left-hand side of the editor. On the tab Pages click the Settings button to the left on the page's title. If you want to enable protection for passwords Go to Permissions, then choose it. Once you've done that, you'll get the option of "Choose Password," where you'll be able to input your password. Then, select your preferred language, then click the"Finish" button. Make a note of your password in a place where you will be able to quickly find it. You might want to restrict access to certain parts of your website only to members and customers paying only.

Wix dashboard

The dashboard on Wix is the very first page you'll be presented with when you sign into your account. It's the hub to all your internet properties. If you're managing only one site this isn't as important however it becomes efficient when managing multiple websites. The page can be accessed through the editor. Select the section (located on the left uppermost) and then My Sites.

Templates, sites as well as subscriptions can all be managed from the dashboard. The same is true for Newsletters, site histories as well as apps.

Selecting a domain name for a name

If you want to create a site with Wix You can use an subdomain.Wix.com. If you'd like the idea, you can also opt to buy your domain. Domain registration is inexpensive, using this option to personalize your site and appearance is a great strategy to build your brand. If you've decided to buy the domain you want, check out the website linked above. Select "Setup with the registrar," then fill in the fields.

Keep your website safe

The site can save at any time through the process. It will be restored in the future. The first step is to go to MySites on Wix.com to view your personal websites. If you make a site using Wix and you're asked to name it that will be the permanent URL. After making any adjustments, click Save on the top of the editor.

Publish

Click the top-right of the editor and select Publish once you are ready to open your site. Do you want to do it over again and press that Publish button? Then, you need to create a domain name for your website then enter it and then click "Save Now" if you did not already. In order to include your domain on your site, you'll need to upgrade to the Premium Plan. Additionally, you'll need purchase an additional part.

It's a great thing to be satisfied with yourself because you've just launched a site! If you're not already created your site, do it now with Wix.

Chapter 7: Overview of WIX

Wix Web Site Builder Wix Web Site Builder a vital instrument that allows users to create their online presence through Drag-and-Drop interfaces. It doesn't require any previous knowledge of coding to begin which makes it an ideal choice for people who are just starting out. Also, newbies do not require prior knowledge for hosting their websites on servers. They just need to have a valid email address. Web design with Wix Builder is quick, easy, and affordable which makes it perfect for small and new enterprises. You don't have to be afraid to launch your Wix site. This complete guide will provide users with everything they need to build the perfect site. Making a website on Wix may seem overwhelming initially. But, Wix is well-recognized as user-friendly. So you are able to take your time and relax. Make your brand and promote yourself, or create an online e-commerce powerful tool with this instructional guide on the best way to utilize Wix to build a stylish web site.

When you're ready to begin development, you may choose between the WxEditor and the WxApiDeveloperInterface (ADI) as your website builder. Both are simple to utilize. But there's a important distinction between them when you're looking for standard builders Wix Editor is the best option, as it lets you choose your templates and build it using simple drag-and-drop processes. With ADI the user doesn't need to be concerned about the construction process because we take care of everything by using the power from artificial intelligence. Answer just a couple of questions, and the program can create your website for you. Content and pages on websites are, naturally, its primary feature. The Wix platform provides you with the basic features of a home page blogs, and a shop, that you are able to modify in real-time. It is possible to include as many pages you wish through the normal Add Click the gear on the Wix dashboard. You can access the Page button. You can also erase the page. When you make real-time modifications to your webpages it will save you having to keep checking and revising the work you've done before it's released. Additionally, you do not have to search for an "save" button because Wix does it for you instantly.

If you've created the basic pages, you can improve your website's performance by adding useful apps. Wix's Wix app store is full of applications that you are able to select and add to your site that range from e-commerce marketing, to managing your site. For a quick search of what you're searching for, browse popular products using the search function, or pick a certain area.

Wix pricing strategies

The pros and pros and

Pros

Offers a no-cost plan that is not time-bound.

Every premium plan comes with an unpaid domain as well as an SSL certificate.

The choices available will satisfy the needs of a large majority of clients.

Cons

The price increases when you purchase the top merchandise

There could be numerous plans to track.

Comparison of Wix packages

The fees per month for Wix are based on the following: Wix can range from zero to forty-nine bucks. Five of these plans were made for normal websites. The remaining three plans are premium eCommerce packages that permit sellers to market online and give you the tools to succeed.

The Wix website's program

Websites that are normal with Wix are priced from 0 dollars per month up to 39 dollars per month. Apart from one plan that is free, the remaining plans are four. Wix general plans include the domain free for one year, removal of advertisements on Wix and the use of an SSL certificate with no extra fee. We'll take a look at these plans.

Free-of-cost plan

It is possible to get this plan without cost, but it comes with too many restrictions for it to serve as a viable web site. Actually, Wix's free trial is a better title. The features you can expect with this free trial includes:

500MB storage and bandwidth

Subdomain ending in ".wixsite.com."

Wx Advertisement on Every Page

Wx Fav in URL

Wx Fav in URL

The free Wix plan is an excellent alternative if you're wanting to try out the waters. But, the other features will require an upgrade, unless you're comfortable using Wix's logo as well as small storage space on your website. The cost per month for the Combo package is $16.00. The package includes all essentials to create personal websites such as blogs as well as additional projects. For a better understanding of what you can expect I'll list these points:

The option to create an individual domain

A domain name that is free for one year

the elimination of Wix advertising

No cost SSL certificate

2. Two gigabytes worth of bandwidth

Three gigabytes storage space

Thirty-minutes of video

In general, Combo only provides a limited amount of resources particularly in the area of storage. But, the information it offers is sufficient for an easy starter site that can be used for personal portfolios.

Unlimited

At only $18.00/month, Unlimited is perfect for solopreneurs, start-ups and freelance contractors.

What you receive with Unlimited is:

Free SSL certificate with unlimited bandwidth

10GB storage

1 hour video

The Site Booster software is one of the many benefits that you'll get when signing to Bluehost. Add a personal domain for free and also get a new one for a whole year.

This plan is perfect for websites with smaller sites that require more power than is accessible within Como. Unlimited removes the bandwidth limit and boosts the capacity of storage.

Pro

The professional plan offered by Wix cost $23.00 per month. It is ideal for media-rich sites, or for those that are in need of a wealth of resources, but do not have the capabilities of e-commerce.

It includes:

Unlimited bandwidth and Storage space (20 GB)

You can add a customized domain at no cost for the duration of a year.

Remove Wix ads

Free logo maker. website booster for free, no cost user analytics and a no-cost app to create an event calendar for a calendar per year

Simply put, Wix professional, which comes with an larger storage limits and extended time for uploading videos it is an excellent option for managing media-rich websites, such as photography, videography or even design. Also, its logo designer and Calendar of Events app could prove useful on businesses-focused sites.

VIP

At a cost at $39 per month this plan offers by far the best and most costly option available for all Wix plans. It's a lot like that of the Pro plan, it has a couple of minor enhancements such as more storage space and higher upload limits for video and more efficient customer service.

The inclusions in the VIP plan are:

The possibility of adding the custom domain of your choice, an unpaid domain for a year, the elimination of Wix advertisements and unlimited bandwidth. 35GB of storage and five minutes of videos, no-cost logo creator and website booster for free (along with a creator of videos) include all of this plan from Wix.

Overall the prices offered by Wix are reasonable when you look at the overall plan. Although the builder doesn't have the greatest amount of the resources available, particularly in terms of storage however, it's nevertheless in the market. Furthermore, Wix can make up for shortages in resources by offering other capabilities.

Chapter 8: Basic Business

The Basic plan is the most affordable online shopping package Wix has available and costs $23.00 each month. Wix is a reliable e-commerce platform which includes everything you'll need to begin selling your products online.

The Strategy is comprised of the following elements:

Paying online and generating sales via social media platforms, or setting up recurring payment plans are all options that can be considered for companies in today's world.

The ability to register your domain online

Domain name that you can customize for one year at no cost with Wix ads removed and a free SSL certificate Unlimited bandwidth, 20GB of storage, five minutes of videos etc.

Basic is ideal for small online stores as well as local brick-and-mortar businesses that require the capabilities of e-commerce.

Business Unlimited

For $27.00/month Business Unlimited, a service offered by Wix is among the most sought-after plans for firms. The plan includes everything you'll need to get selling online, and is a step up from that of the Business Basic Plan in terms of support tools and software.

The items included in Business Unlimited Business Unlimited package are the following:

It is a possibility to accept online transactions, selling through social media platforms, setting up recurring payments, as well as offering subscription

Numerous Currencies

Better shopping and drop-off methods

There are no limits on quotas and the supply is endless

Create a customized domain name to the functionality of.

The domain that you design is for sale for a year.

The Deletion of Ads on Wix

Free SSL Certificates

Unlimited bandwidth

Capacity 35GB

Ten hours of playback video

This is the ideal Strategy for a majority of businesses that are committed to selling their products on the internet. This storage space can be used to host many products on your site.

VIP business

Business VIP priced at $49.00 per month. This is WX's highest priced plan. It's the ideal choice for those who require a large amount in storage (which is very typical in online retail) or a priority support for customers.

Accepting payments online as well as selling subscriptions, creating the recurring payment system, as well as marketing via social media platforms is made possible by these options. Additionally, there are various currencies, advanced search and buying choices, Limitless items, the possibility to create the option of a custom domain, customized domain free for a year, removing Wix advertisements and Free SSL certification with unlimited bandwidth, 50GB of storage space, unlimited hours of video, and priority customer support are offered in this package.

This program is intended to supply online store owners with an extensive set of e-commerce and business tools with priority support, as well as ample storage space. In the end, it's clear that Wix's pricing for e-commerce is in line with the industry average. Wix's structure is more luxurious that its rivals, but. Furthermore, the builder has the largest options of designs available.

What Wix program should I choose?

The plans offered by Wix tend to be classified into two groups one for smaller or normal businesses and ones designed specifically for online shops. If you are looking for a good option for their small or personal website there are five plans you can consider. But, the variety could seem overwhelming and every plan is created equally.

Best Website Design for a Personal or Small Business

The Combo package is the best choice if you are planning to use anything other than E-commerce functions. With the cost you will get enough tools to manage your portfolio, blog, or a lean website for business. There are three distinct plans to run online stores when you decide to utilize Wix to sell products online. All plans have a lot of features and are appropriate for businesses that operate online There is a plan that meets the demands for the majority of clients.

The best strategy for an eCommerce site

If you're looking to get the most of your internet selling, Business Unlimited is the place to begin. It comes with the most essential E-commerce capabilities and features, and adequate storage resources for small to moderate-sized online store.

Additional cost for Wix

As with many other platforms for developers, Wix is comprehensive in that it comes with all you require, which includes hosting, a no-cost domain name and one SSL certificate, a site builder and much other features. In the end, there's no pricing comparable to those of other Wix account for email. However, this is a welcome information as it will cut down unnecessary expenses. But, you could still incur some long-term costs, like domain registrations as well as app purchase and transaction costs.

Domain name

The paid Wix plans include the option of a domain free for a year. After the first year is over but, renewal fees will be required. If you're searching for a brand new domain it is recommended to choose another site than Wix because of its steep cost. Pricing starts at $14.95 annually for the most common TLDs. Connecting a domain that is hosted on another company is an alternative to Wx's expensive cost for registration of a domain. As an example, HostGator charges $9.99 annually for an basic.com TLD. GoDaddy is charged $11.99. Namecheap is even cheaper as annual costs start with $7.98.

Wix Ascend Pricing

Wix Ascend is the builder's single-stop solution to automate emails and social media, SEO leads, email marketing, and many more features for business. The prices for this integrated service start at a low of zero dollar per month, and can go upwards to an affordable cost of $49. There are four distinct Ascend plans. The benefits you receive with the plans is according to:

There are four Advance plans that are available. The information that comes with each one of them follows:

The free version permits the use of up to five forms with 10 fields on each form, three campaigns per month and 5 000 monthly mailers. Furthermore, the program raises the bar for brand and chatbox of the campaign and two active automations as well as a the monthly output on social media comprising three posts.

The basic plan ($10/month) You get 10 forms, with unlimitted fields, five campaign per month, with an maximum of 9500 monthly messages, deletion of Ascend brand out of your chatbox and campaigns, as well as seven automatic reminders.

You receive 20 forms throughout the life of your site that are unlimited in fields, 20 campaigns each month, with the possibility of 10,000 monthly messages, deletion of Ascend branding in your chatbox and campaigns, the ability to access five team members, as well as 20 forms per completion. The Professional plan is $29 monthly.

Unlimited ($49/month) covers endless forms and campaigns that can reach a an maximum of 1 million monthly emails and the elimination of Ascend branding in the chatbox and campaigns with unlimitless team members, active automating, posts on social media as well as ad elimination.

If you are looking to make the maximum benefit from Ascend You must upgrade to at a minimum the basic plan. For the best experience of Ascend You must upgrade at a minimum to the basic plan.

Wix App Market

It's best that you have no issues in keeping your website functioning with Wix because it's completely self-sufficient. But, in order to make the most of the features of Wix, you'll have to purchase third-party applications available on Wix App Market. Wix App Market. Additionally, a vast range of extensions is available priced between free and hundreds of dollars each month within the Wix marketplace. Like, Google AdSense is available without cost. But the price of making use of QuickBooks Sync is $129 per month. If you wish to take advantage of all options, you'll have put aside a couple of dollars each month.

Wix is not charged any charges for transaction processing or transactions for its services. But, you could incur transaction costs making use of Wix Payments. You can transfer money to the builder, with no fee related. There is you will be charged a Wix processing charge is applied to all gateway payment. The location of your purchase determines the exact Wix cost of payment. U.S.A.: 2.9% of purchase price plus $0.30

Canada: 2.9% of the purchase price plus CAD 0.30

The fee is 2.1 percent of the total purchase cost for the United Kingdom, plus 0.20 GBP.

EU countries: 1.90% of the purchase price plus 0.30 EUR

Switzerland: 2.3% of the total amount plus 0.30 CHF

Additionally, PayPal, Stripe, and Apple Pay Additional payment integrations are also offered. But, each of these methods come with similar fees to those that of Wix Payments platform.

Chapter 9: Tips for pricing on Wix

Select an annual billing cycle as well as a different domain registrar. You can skip the premium options, make use of the virtual private network and save on costs with Wix. Pick the annual billing cycle and Annual Plan option for greatest savings. Combo For instance, it includes a fee of $19 per month. If you choose to sign up for the entire year's worth of service in one go, the monthly cost will be $16. Compare prices to find the best price in the event that you have for you to renew the domain the first year is up. Below is a quick overview of the typical cost.

Different providers offer the.com highest-level domain annual cost for Wx costs $14.95.

To sign up to Hottinger You must purchase $9.99 per year.

The fee for the annual subscription for Godaddy amounts to $11.99.

The annual cost to use Namecheap will be $7.98.

The Cut features on Extra Apps

Wix is highly knowledgeable. So, there shouldn't be any difficulty removing any third-party applications in order to cut costs. But, it's recommended to use the free app instead of the paid ones. Pricing for Wix is different based the region you reside in; make use of the VPN (VPN) to find out if some regions have lower prices. A 12-month contract with Unlimited within the United States would set you for $18.00 each month. Likewise, an unlimited subscription in Malaysia is only going to cost $12.50 each month. This is where you need a virtual private networks (VPN) solution such as Nordvpn is a great option. Take advantage of the numerous discounts offered by WX. It offers up to 50% off on new customers. There is also 50% off for students. Be conscious that there's not a specific "Wix non-profit pricing." But, there are a number of methods to lower Wix prices to be affordable level.

Wix vs Competitive Pricing

Wix isn't the most affordable site builder on the market. Additionally, if you're seeking a quick solution, the adaptability of Wix could become too difficult to manage. Dependence on third-party software could be frustrating at times. It's good to know that there are many reliable substitute site developers are offered through Zyro as well as Squarespace.

Pricing in Wix and Zyro

If you've decided that Wix doesn't suit your needs then your alternative will be Zyro. Zyro is a popular building platform that offers its users numerous benefits, including vast resources, low cost as well as simple control options, along with numerous useful integrations.

Zyro vs Wix: Which Is Better for Personal Websites?

Zyro's Unleashed ($2.69/mo) vs Wix's Unlimited ($18/mo). Both plans offer a free domain name for a year, as well as an SSL certificate with unlimited bandwidth, among additional benefits. Zyro's Unleashed is nearly 4 times more affordable than WX's Limitless however, it only has ten gigabytes storage as opposed to Zyro's infinite storage on it's Unlimited plan.

Differences Between Zyro and Wix for E-Commerce Websites

Zyro's eCommerce service (at $8.01/month) will be contrasted with the Wix Business Unlimited plan (at

$27/month). Both plans are completely free of costs or commissions. But, Zyro's eCommerce platform must catch up with Wix's features offered in Business Unlimited. The e-commerce service of Zyro is still a strong competitor because it is nearly three times less expensive and offering many more options. As opposed the Wix's Business Unlimited, which caps storage to 35GB, Zyro's online-commerce plans do not include this limit.

Pricing for Wx and Squarespace.

The other competitor to Wix's premium plans is Squarespace. It is a popular builder that draws customers with gorgeous templates, extensive features, and advanced methods of marketing.

For creating a website for your personal use You can pick from Squarespace or Wix.

They offer entry plans that are suitable for personal websites for individual websites.

The plan offered by Squarespace is priced at just $16 a month, and Wix's Business plan is exactly the same per month. Both plans offer the SSL certificate, as well as a free domain name for a year. But when it comes to storage and bandwidth the limits are not there for the Personal edition of Squarespace. However, the Wix Combo comes with data transfer limitations that are 2GB in size and storage limit of 3GB.

Comparison of Squarespace with Wix to create e-commerce websites.

In terms of e-commerce options, Squarespace Business ($18.00/month) and Wix Business Basic ($23.00/month) are the best options with the lowest prices per month. In this package, you are able to accept online payment as well as have unlimited bandwidth. the use of a domain free for one year, as well as a complimentary SSL certificate. While Wix's Business Basic plan only provides 20GB of storage. The latter is superior in this regard. Additionally, there are none transaction charges for Wix's Business Basic as opposed to Squarespace's Business Basic, which costs 3 percent. Additionally, Wix'dz Business Basic offers the most advanced features in e-commerce as well as subscription sales as well as marketing via social media. In conclusion, Zyro and Squarespace are two great alternatives to Wix. Don't expect perfect results from any builder Each has its benefits and drawbacks.

How much will it cost to get a website designed by Wx?

The cost for a year of an Wix website is contingent on the features you select and could vary from 0 dollars to forty-nine dollars a month.

What amount of cost is Wix charge for every transaction?

Wix does not charge fee for transactions. But, it is crucial to keep in mind that additional processing charges may be required in accordance with your selected payment method.

Do I qualify for free payments with this plan? Wix plan?

Because all payment processors charge fee for transactions, taking payments through Wix is not free.

Do I have the ability to use my domain's name using WX?

Wix provides a free domain for the first year. When you sign up with Wix you can make use of the domain you have registered.

How often do Wix organize sale events?

Wix is often offering discounts throughout the year, and especially around major holidays, like Black Friday.

Chapter 10: How to Sign Up for Wix and Create Your First Website

Visit www.Wix.com and Click "Get Started"

With Wix it is possible to begin developing your site immediately and not worry about the technological infrastructure. It's important to take a moment to explain how to do it:

First, you should know about collaboration with Wix. One of the advantages about working with Wix is that you are able to build your website for no cost and decide later whether or not you want to move to a paid service. First, visit the Wix's main Wix site, click on the button to get started after which you can sign for a Free Account to start. After that, enter the details of your contact and click the"Sing up" button. After that, you'll be directed to Wix for Wix ADI (Artificial Intelligence Designer).

Press the Let's Get It button to start.

Wix will inquire about your needs prior to configuring your website with optimal settings, based on the answers you provide.

The question at the beginning is simple:

The most likely scenario is that "myself" is what you'll pick in this box.

The third question is about the type of website you're planning to build and, as you'll notice there are a variety of options. It is important to take this action because it's vital. Based on your input, Wix will automatically optimize your site for SEO. Because business websites are popular, this is the type that we'll concentrate on in this article. These questions can help to distill the core of your website in just one phrase.

Pisk When the first questions are answered, Wix will ask whether you've got enough confidence in the ADI to build an example website or to create it by hand. If you choose to use the ADI it is possible to come back to tweak the design of your website later to ensure maximum effectiveness. It is not only limited by the initial recommendations of WX.

You can initiate the process by pressing the button Get Moving.

Based on the answers that you gave just a few seconds back, Wix will ask you a few questions that will help decide on the ideal style and layout that will meet your needs.

1. The very first thing that we must know is what type of company you'd like the website to be designed to serve. Be aware that if you select another option at the first step, for instance, "online store" instead of "business site"--Wix provides an

array of choices. When you start entering your business's definition Wix will give you a variety of options. In the example above, when we type "massage," Wix has the following suggestions:

This display is to serve the reason of showing how diverse types of business exist. The site is powered by Wix and also offers templates and examples of code. We've settled to "Massage Therapy" as the design theme of the demonstration site we're working on.

Clisk after you've narrowed in on the business or web design that is most effectively for you, proceed to step 2.

Wix will suggest a selection of functions for your site depending on the selections that you've made up to now. For our case, Wix recommends a module to allow chat, books on the internet as well as a blog as well as a variety of other features. The information you will see in this page is based on the answers you give. Make sure you check the boxes beside the options that are appropriate to the needs of your website when you look through the list.

The next step is Wix soliciting specific information regarding your business to be used for the domain name for your site. It is possible to use your own name when creating a site for your business. In order to continue, Wix will inquire whether there is already any existing online material that you can import into your brand new Wix website. Imports of other websites as well as Google Places listings are also available in Wix. Importing information from other sites can be risky and must be avoided as much as feasible. Next, click.

You can now choose an attractive design for your site on Wix.

To make the decision-making process as straightforward as is possible, Wix starts you out with some pre-designed designs instead of a wall with hundreds of possibilities. There are several options that you can choose from, and the outcome is contingent on what you choose to answer. We will first give you a filtering template list that matches the style you prefer. We, for instance, believe that"Breeze" style is a good choice "Breeze" style is fine for massage therapists, however, ultimately the choice is entirely yours. Once you've made your choice the style you prefer, Wix offers a variety of accurate options for your homepage. Based on your prior selections, the websites will be already populated with relevant images and designed in a specific manner.

What it says is that there's a lot of pictures that relate to sexual assaults in these sites. We don't put the images on purpose. This is Wix's best chance to anticipate which pages will help me and my business. Select the website that interests your most. Make Your Site Personal Site When you've chosen the homepage you'll be directed on to your Wix ADI editor. There, you'll be able to alter your site's appearance and choose which features you want to add.

It could be something similar to this:

Every aspect of this site behaves just as you'd hope it would as it's extremely simple to use. You can, for instance, choose the text, then hit"Edit" or click "Edit" button to edit an individual section of text in the webpage. The menu will be a fresh panel from which you can edit the content. In this case, we selected the block (which is "Wyatt Collier") listed below. The toolbar came up, which allowed me to modify the name as well as include a subtitle as well as a brief description.

When you click one of the blocks listed on the homepage, you'll be taken to a editing interface, in which you can alter the information contained in that particular block. Below is a sample of the work we've done in our "My Treatments" section. Each text section edits itself and then the text can be refined in tandem. Don't worry regarding losing work as Wix ADI editor automatically saves your work. Wix ADI editor will automatically save. The customization of your designs isn't restricted to just changing one or two words in a few places.

Revising the Segments

It is the Wix ADI editor enables you to arrange your page's parts by simply dragging and dropping it, as well as altering the structure of your document by changing the various sections. When you look at one part there are two arrows icons within the upper left corner of the page. The arrows let you lift and lower a particular section. These sections will organize them in a snap if you click them. Alongside changing the contents of your sections, you are able to change their appearance through switching their style of design. As an example, when you move the mouse over"My Treatments," in "My Treatments" section, an icon labeled "Design" appears in the right-hand side of your screen. If you click on it, a new screen opens with designs from which you choose.

Select the model you like and switch the one you have with just one click.

The modification of the sections that are already in place is a good thing, however it is also possible to add complete new sections.

For this, visit the menu at the top and select the button to add, and then select "Section to Page."

There are a variety of categories and topics to pick from. The sections are organized already in order to simplify things:

You can drag and drop any portion of the sidebar on the right-hand panel. This is how a page that has testimonials sections will look like in a sample:

Pick the one you like to replace the one you have in one click.

The ability to alter the sections that are already in place is a good thing, but it is also possible to add sections that are completely new. For this, head to the menu at the top and select the Add button and then select "Section to Page."

There are a variety of subjects and sections to pick from. The sections have been organized in order to simplify things:

You can drag and drop any portion of the sidebar on the right-hand panel. This is how a page that has a section for testimonials will look like in a sample:

It is obvious that everything in that testimonial section as well as its text could be improved.

The Wix Editor for ADI provides users with the default colour scheme and font setting at the time you start using the software. These will work in the majority of scenarios, but if prefer a more refined look, it's easy to swap them.

To accomplish this, click Design from the menu. Then, click Colors in the menu.

This is also where Wix goes above and beyond to help you with the process. As an example, instead of showing thousands of colors It simply asks you which colour you prefer for your Design upon. Then, it provides suggestions for color combinations that complement each other.

Select your preferred seed color.

Select the color scheme you want to use (toned or vibrant, vivid and dark or a mixture of all).

Choose one of the colors.

The entire color scheme could take some time.

The same way Your fonts should receive the same respect. Click on the menu's Design tab and select from the Fonts option.

Wix offers a range of ideas once more.

It's ideal to keep going around and round between choices until you have found one you love. It is recommended that you used the font size tool in order to ensure that the content displayed on your website is understandable.

Enhancing the Visual Appeal by Including Pictures, Slideshows, and Other Visual Elements

If you have a website Wix can take any type of graphic content. If you're looking to publish slideshows, photos, videos galleries or Instagram feeds Wix is able to take care of it.

We'll start with basics like including images to your website or updating your existing ones.

If you wish to change images, click the appropriate section, then choose Edit & Replace from the Sidebar.

When you hit the button, Wx will open you to a brand new window, where you are able to make additional modifications to the photo.

To change your image, just click on"Replace" on the Replace button. There's a chance to see Wix offers a variety of images with the same basic idea. These images can be used for your website without having to worry about violating anyone else's copyrights. Upload your photo select it, then hit on the "+ Upload Media" button located in the upper left hand corner. After the upload has completed it is possible to make modifications to the photo.

Once you're done then select "Apply" to see the image on the screen.

If you want to add new media select it using the Add button on the top menu. Then choose the appropriate category in the different submenus. It's like adding a brand new playlist or album. If you want to rearrange your media files, simply click within the block in the same way and then select Edit & Replace.

Maximize Your Site's Potential on Mobile Devices

Today mobile phones are frequently the only option for Internet access. The number of people who use mobile phones is higher than laptop or desktop computers together. It is crucial to make sure that your site displays properly when viewed on mobile devices. Users will go elsewhere when you do not succeed in the first place, and will probably never come back.

In addition that mobile's impact increases as you realize that you're most likely operating a business in the local area. Keywords that include "near me" account for the majority of all local traffic that Google receives and therefore, being able to quickly serve those users is vital for you to attract the attention of these users. Think about yourself as the person in control of the massage similar to the parlor mentioned earlier. If a person searches in the search engine for "massage near me" and your site pops up but the site doesn't show on their mobile, the prospective customer will not visit your site.

You can quickly and effortlessly transform your website to be mobile-friendly making use of Wix.

For the first step, select an alternative perspective by pressing on the appropriate button located in the upper bar.

It will refresh the webpage and show what it looks like on mobile devices.

The website you have created should appear excellent right from the box, however there's always an opportunity to improve. Changes are made in order to highlight essential elements while minimizing those that aren't so important.

Importantly, your changes do not alter the display on desktops of your website. For mobile phones only, you must.

Below are a few suggestions you can take to boost the mobile user experience on your website:

Hide pictures not essential, and they only fill up space in the view on mobile devices.

Add your contact information up to at the top.

Use a responsive design.

It is possible to make changes to your website by using Wix such as hiding certain elements and changing the layout of sections. Maximize your visit and satisfaction. Once you're done, can easily go back to the desktop. Any changes you make are automatically saved.

Chapter 11: Make Some New Content

After the homepage is complete We can now move to the other pages that most websites require. The first step is to create there is an "About" and "Contact" page. In the meantime this article, we'll use these two instances to demonstrate fundamental page design techniques.

About page

For the first step, go to the webpage the HOME BUTTON which is located at the SECOND LEFT CORNER. Click on"+ Add Page" "+ Add Page" button.

Wx gives suggestions on typical page formats that you might consider useful. First, obviously the About page.

Wx suggests pages that which you can build, and offers pre-made layouts of each page.

To complete your About page, look through the collection of design options and pick that one you love the best.

The Wix ADI Editor will refresh the interface, allowing you to work on the new "About page".

The insides and outs of how things work can be found on the home page.

Edit your content to ensure it should be on your About page.

Just a few minutes of your time could create an amazing "About page".

Contact Us Page

Making a Contact page can be like creating a Contact page, however it has distinct features. To begin, simply click the Page button, and follow add a page by clicking the Add button. You can then test the Wix messaging options by changing to Contact. Choose one of the suggested designs. You will see that the Wix ADI editing interface will refresh. There are some distinct sections that don't appear found on your About page, or your homepage. Thodze include:

Wx suggests adding a contact form as well as an interactive map of the contact page in order to make it easier for customers' journeys to your company. Contact form is fully operational, and therefore visitors to your site could use it to get in touch to your company.

NOTE: If you're not a company and do not want to share your address, it is possible to remove the map, and then continue with the contact form.

Other pages that are specific to niches based on the first answers that you submitted when you signed in with Wix You may find other pages in your site which have been designed by Wix.

We've got an Books Online page and a Readings Checklist page. Verify the state of your website by hitting the Page button at the top left corner.

Please review the formatting of the pages, and then make any changes you think are necessary. The basic principles are the same.

Fine-tuning Site Navigation By default

The new pages you have created are included in your website's main navigation bar.

If you want to rearrange menu options, visit the site's header and press the Edit button on the right side of MENU to reorder the items in the order you prefer.

You can rearrange the pages by moving and dropping them back into their original positions.

If you would like to connect to sites that are not part of your site (such like your profile on social media) it is possible to add it manually menu items.

Include a Blog (Optional)

A blog is a fantastic method to connect with a larger readership and to convert them to customers who pay. According to research, blogging is among the most efficient digital marketing tools that businesses have in the present. People who focus on blogging are thirteen times more likely to earn positive returns of investment (ROI) via their activities online over those who do not.

If you wish to get users to be drawn to your website, it is important to give them an incentive to visit your site. As an example, blogging can be beneficial if the information your site provides is top-quality and is able to satisfy the requirements and desires of your targeted viewers.

In terms of technology making a blog with Wix is straightforward as you already have all the tools you need.

For creating a brand new page on the Wix blog. Wix blog.

Select Pages from the main menu, and then select + Add Page. Select Blog in the drop-down menu. select a layout for your blog which appeals to your.

The exact layout is up to you. One of these options will accomplish just fine! It's as simple as that! Wix editor will refresh the page, allowing you to see your blog's page updated working.

This page will be modified just like any other page of your website can be edited. The most important thing is that you are able to change the layout of the blog (where photographs are placed and so on.) as well as how your blog posts are displayed on the site.

Change the information in relation to the posts (author dates, the author's name, etc.).

You can write your own blog entries and also take care of the ones you already have.

Posting New Content to a Blog

To visit on the Management Blog, go to the main Blog page.

You are able to manage existing posts as well as start new ones on this page.

Its interface is similar in appearance to that similar to that of Microsoft Word. You can choose between Microsoft Word or the Google Docs word processor.

What you will get are the following:

Integrated Search Engine Optimization Tools - to Ensure Your Posts Appear on Google

Advanced Text Editor

Format and tags

Access to a vast collection of authors with a wide range of talents

Great mobile experience

Personalized HTML Support

Include an E-Commerce Site (Voluntary)

This shouldn't come as a surprise that launching a store online store on Wix is doable in a short time. Additionally, it'll function as a completely functional online shop that doesn't limit you to any restrictions.

A vast array of goods is readily available for you.

Create your own shopfront design and a shopping cart.

Promote tangible as well as digital products.

Look for an order.

Place in place charges for shipping.

Pay over the Internet.

Promote your business via social media platforms such as Facebook as well as Instagram.

Keep track of the sales you make wherever you are using this app. Wix App.

Using Wix to Make a Virtual Store

Choose Pages from the main menu and select + Add Pages. The drop-down menu will let you select Online Store and pick a layout that appeals to your.

Select the "Store" tab and then "Manage Products" to make modifications to your inventory, and modify product descriptions.

The new interface appear in which you are able to add new products modify their descriptions, prices, etc.

We're not going to provide additional details about how to build an online store that is successful because that's what's in this instruction. The main goal of this guide was to show how simple it can be to start an online store with Wix. Wix offers every option you could need.

Find out What the main Wix Dashboard looks like The dashboard we've seen so far is using the Wix ADI, and all it can do through it. It's quite a bit. But, a stand-alone Wix dashboard is available at your fingertips. It's designed to give you an overall overview of your site's various parameters. You must log off and then go back to Wx in order to gain an access point to your dashboard. It will look something similar to the following:

Let's break the content on this page into parts:

This is the primary sidebar that you are able to quickly navigate through various areas on your website. If you manage blogs or have an online store, you can see sections that manage your items, blog posts, orders and reservations. Additionally, there are links to related resources including web pages as well as mobile applications. Below you'll find an edit button that takes you to the exact Wix ADI editor that we've been using.

The main user interface to manage your site. This is where you can select any tasks that are related to your site you wish to accomplish.

A brief introduction to the concept. Make sure to follow these steps in order to ensure that your site is prepared for the arrival of guests.

More information about using your website can be located in the block below the page.

Another place to examine can be the Settings menu. It can be accessible from the main menu. You can modify a variety of elements of your site like its name, general details, the integration to other platforms such as payment options, currencies as well as more. However it is still recommended to explore your options to see what's on the market even if you do not change anything.

Enhance the Usage through Wix Apps

If you feel that the tools offered by Wix do not meet your needs You can explore Wix App Market Wix App Market for more alternatives. More than 200 applications can assist you in creating and expanding your site.

Apps can be accessed via the Apps option in the main page in Wix's dashboard. Wix dashboard.

There's an application for almost everything you could imagine. All the way from SEO (search engine optimization) (SEO) for live chats, email newsletters pop-ups that integrate social media with and split-testing cart abandonment, tools for cart abandonment, contacts managers and much more.

The process of adding apps is as simple as several steps. Click on the Add Application button when you want to add an app to the listing.

Some additional configuration is required, based on the program you've picked.

Just Pick a Pricing Strategy and Get Started. Your Site

The website you have created is near completion. It's out for the world to see. There are some things you'll require...

For publishing your website Go to your Wix ADI Editor (click on the Edit Site button on the Wx dashboard's lower left corner) then click the large blue Publish button.

You'll have to choose whether you want to utilize Wix's free Wix subdomain or to connect to a domain that you have created.

Prior to making this choice take a look at the cost of various Wix plans. Your decision to select a specific plan will determine the choice of your domain name.

The first thing to note is that you can get a totally free account with Wix. It is limited to Wix's basic Wix subdomain. You can't connect to a domain that you have created. Wix ads will be displayed all over your site. You're only allowed 500MB storage.

If you are in agreement with the above restrictions then you can proceed by choosing the subdomain for free illustrated in the picture. The site is operational and ready to welcome users at this time.

However should these limits prove excessively restrictive, you'll have to purchase the more expensive premium plans. Make use of the mouse to select one of the Upgrade options in the display.

Choose a price structure which is most suitable for your needs. There are two kinds of plans available:

If you are only looking to create a basic site using Wix (no web-based store, or any other aspect that requires your customers to pay to use the website) The costs will be according to the following.

Are you looking to make sales on our site? This Business Basics plan is the highest value, at only $33 per month. Everything you need to be successful in online selling is provided.

Only interested in having great personal data or even a blog? Go with the Limitless plan and pay one-time payment of $17.

If these aren't the cheapest plans available, what is the reason we recommend these plans? Simple; you could always upgrade to something more expensive at a later date.

If you opt for one of our packages, then you'll be able to get the domain name free in the beginning of your first year! If you are choosing a domain you should choose a name that's suitable and memorable to your brand or company is ideal.

If you've upgraded your plan to one of the premium plans, and have completed the purchasing process the site will become available and ready for use by businesses.

Chapter 12: Apply These Wx Tricks to Elevate Your Web Design

Scroll effect of the picture.

The different parts of your site should be able to perform differently. There's a trick you can apply to make things go through an extra boost. Display a static image on one side while scrolling text is displayed on the other.

Here's how:

Launch Wix Editor. Open Wix Editor and then click "Add" on the left edge of the screen. add the strip.

You can go to "Layouts" and divide the screen into two columns: one on the left, and one to the right (you can also choose to automatically divided into two columns with equal size).

Include two additional columns beneath in the same size.

Backgrounds for columns are customizable via pressing "Change Strip Background" and selecting an appropriate picture or the desired the desired text.

Select the effect scroll "Reveal" in the "Settings" for the column you want to make it more prominent on that side. Repeat this procedure to the column beneath. The scrolling effect as shown below that is, the image appears to stay static while the text changes with each scroll.

Pay attention to how the text appears to shift when you scroll. However, that image to left stays still.

Dual-speed scrolling

Are you looking to keep your viewers interested? Explore exposing your pictures by themselves and stacking them up in various arrangements. Use parallax and reveal to produce the illusion of multi-layered scrolling.

How do you:

Add two strips over one another in the arrangement you prefer.

The trip can be made to appear as if it was a film set by personalizing the backgrounds.

Choose"Reveal" scroll effect "Reveal" scroll effect in the "Settings" menu for a one-time journey, and then use the "Parallax" effect for another. This is because the pictures appear to move at different rates.

Certain templates on websites have elements that move at different speeds. This tutorial will show you the basics you require how to make the effects.

Slideshow with animated graphics

Show your work in an engaging manner. You can, for instance, mix images that are static, superimposed on an animated slideshow that showcases your finest works. Try experimenting with different filtering options on the same image for an interesting end result.

How do you:

Create a slideshow using "Add" and then "Interactive."

Click "Change Slide Background," and then, in "Settings," select "Tile" for the image's size.

Select "Move Slides" from the menu. This will create a duplicate of the slide. Choose "Autoplay upon loading," "Horizontal," and "Right" under "Settings."

Then, you can add an additional strip. Then, select "Layouts" to divide it into two columns, with an aspect ratio of 20:80.

The background of the smaller column could be set to the images you prefer, but making up only 20 percent of the length.

Scrolling at triple-speed

Do you want to lure your site's customers with an irresistible scrolling experience? This method combines zoom-in parallax and static images to create the illusion that elements are moving at various speed.

What can you do?

Three strips are added, one of them over the other.

Change the background of the trip to suit each particular.

You can set one of the scroll effects in the form of "Zoom in," another to "Parallax," and the third option to "None" in the "Settings" menu, under "Scroll Effects." When you scroll through the page, it'll appear as if they're going at different speed.

Automatically Changing Slideshow

Your visuals worthy of some amazing animation effects. You can create two slideshows that are opposite each other by matching their content in order to enhance each other. Cartoon slide shows run in loops, with number of different sections.

Instructions:

Add a strip of paper that divides the text in two columns: one to the left and another to the right.

Select "Add," "Interactive," and "Slideshow" to attach a slideshow.

Please go through the slides, and modify them if necessary. the slides.

Add animations to each slide show, and adjust the timers according to your preferences.

A looping slide is visualized as a presentation

What better way to illustrate your form or appearance as well as your lettering fashion? With this technique, each letter comes with its own text box that is customized with animation and timing. This means that you can apply the same technique to form letters.

How do you:

Add a text box and write a single letter in each.

Include an illustration within each text box. Adjust the time so that the word, or number flow easily.

This same concept is applied to geometric shapes, by breaking the shapes into pieces and then animating the resultant shape.

The "Reveal" animation effect is helpful if you prefer animating an entire phrase or word.

Hover box illustration

Make your visitors awestruck by incorporating friendly cursor animations for them to use. In particular, you can enhance your designs or text with an effect of hovering.

What can you do?

Create an interactive header by clicking "Add" and "Interactive" from the menu which appears.

The hover boxes can be placed in two states: normal or hover. Play around with the layout of"Hover" by adjusting the layout of "Hover," adjusting the hue and amount of shading.

Secret WX Editor Cheats to improve your site's SEO? Remember the time you saw Chinese take-out containers fold into plates (fun to think about it, isn't it?)? We'd like to offer an equally thrilling experience, divulging secrets to allow editing to be effortless.

Interesting? Because making a site is easy, why not try the idea a try?

Use keyboard shortcuts.

Everybody likes shortcuts, don't they? As with the express train in the New York City Subway, making time is always a popular. If you're not sure what to do when creating a site by using Wix The Wix Editor will make it easy. It offers a variety of shortcuts for use that will increase your efficiency and save your time. Here's a collection of examples that must be copied immediately and copy and paste (Ctrl + C or Ctrl + V):

Ctrl + M (Cmd + M): Navigate between your items.

CTRL + J (Cmd + J) to switch between desktop and mobile views.

Ctrl + D (Cmd. D): Dual or Duplicate

CTRL + Ctrl + (Cmd + P) to view your site prior to.

Ctrl + S (Command + S) to help save your site's page.

Create text-based themes

Each time you create the new text box choosing the dimensions, fonts, and format could cause a lot of trouble. Particularly when you must repeat the process each when you create a new box. For that exact reason, we developed text themes.

How does it perform?

In the first place, you need to provide the text field. In the text box, click Settings > Themes select the appropriate theme and modify the theme to suit your needs. After everything is set it is time to save the theme to be saved for future usage. You want to add a new text box? It's not a problem! Select the previous saved theme that you made, and you're done! The text box that you created is distinct from the one before it.

parts to zoom out and arrange

In the process of creating a website starting from scratch, there will be occasions when all you need is an alternative view. This Zoom Out feature can be extremely useful tool which lets users see the entire website in one glance. This overview lets it is easy to rearrange the layout, add or duplicate sections with just a single click. Zoom out: simply click on the magnifying window at the very top of the WX Editor.

The brand new "Snap to Object" is an awesome tool to have This tool can aid in optimizing your web page's layout. The tool is made to allow people to shift pictures or text with a straight line and keeping a neat and tidy arrangement of your website's components.

Press the shift key while you move the object in any direction you'd like. As an example, you can the text and images should be aligned to form a continuous line.

While holding the Shift button move the object to wherever you'd would like.

Connect a device to the box

Container boxes can be located in the additional panels and are used for a variety of reasons. Text can be used in frames, boxes, or galleries as media. However, they tend to be an easy method to mix various elements, and to neatly make sure your site is in line. When you have many elements into a container it is possible to relocate them all at the same time instead of moving each one independently.

You can go to the Add Panel > Box > Container box fill this in. Then, fill the box with items. You will receive the "Attach to box" message will indicate that this step was successful. All of the items you brought to the container box have been connected.

Benefits and drawbacks of Wix's Websites

Wix provides users with a no-cost option and a premium one to create stunning websites. With more than 10 years of experience in the industry and a variety of benefits and drawbacks to wix sites to consider.

What Are the Benefits of Wix Websites?

You get improved design templates.

Thanks to the drag-and-drop features which WX allows, you will be able to easily create a contemporary website. This allows you to create your own or commercial site on the internet without a huge expenditure. Though some designs are limited by the plan for free, overall the user experience is quick and smooth experience for users.

The interface is user-friendly and easy to use.

There are some more beautiful interfaces for backend use with websites currently, but it's extremely beneficial. Everything needed are, in the most cases, just a couple of mouse clicks away. There are also guidelines and the tools needed to modify themes even with the no-cost plan, so you can make your website match with the style of your company.

You're open to long strategies.

Some web builders bind you into contract terms of 24 or 36 months and you could be stuck with a low-cost premium plan. With WX, however, you won't need to worry about that. Instead, you can test WX for as low at $5 per month, and decide to cancel at any time if you decide to upgrade from the free alternative.

WX will take care of the security of your website without sacrificing speed.

Straight out of the box, WIX websites perform at rates that are higher than the industry standard. Additionally, you do not need to think about security because the site is located by the Wix server. But, you must think about how to design your site and working with the products you bought through their various bundles.

The solution is comprehensive.

If you are experiencing issues on your site for any cause, you have to contact WX WX to receive the support you need. It is not necessary to spend time searching for issues or addressing plug-ins or wires which may have issues. Contact the customer service team via either email, phone or via the FAQ page.

What Drawbacks Are There to Wix Websites?

The basic plan doesn't eliminate ads on your website.